Sew This and That!
13 Quick-to-Make Quilted Projects

Sherri K. Falls

Martingale
Create with Confidence

Sew This and That! 13 Quick-to-Make Quilted Projects
© 2016 by Sherri K. Falls

Martingale®
19021 120th Ave. NE, Ste. 102
Bothell, WA 98011-9511 USA
ShopMartingale.com

Printed in China
21 20 19 18 17 16   8 7 6 5 4 3 2 1

Library of Congress Cataloging-in-Publication Data
is available upon request.

ISBN: 978-1-60468-787-3

MISSION STATEMENT

We empower makers who use fabric and yarn
to make life more enjoyable.

CREDITS

PUBLISHER AND
CHIEF VISIONARY OFFICER
Jennifer Erbe Keltner

CONTENT DIRECTOR
Karen Costello Soltys

DESIGN MANAGER
Adrienne Smitke

MANAGING EDITOR
Tina Cook

PRODUCTION MANAGER
Regina Girard

ACQUISITIONS EDITOR
Karen M. Burns

PHOTOGRAPHER
Brent Kane

TECHNICAL EDITOR
Beth Bradley

ILLUSTRATOR
Missy Shepler

COPY EDITOR
Melissa Bryan

contents

introduction

· · · · · · · · · · · · · · · · · ·

There's something so irresistible about small and quick-to-sew projects. When life is busy and I'm short on creative time, it's wonderfully satisfying to finish a project to decorate my home or give to someone special. I designed the patterns in this book with that feeling of accomplishment in mind. From tote bags to quilted table toppers to pillows to zippered pouches, each project is quick and easy enough to complete in a short amount of time.

I also designed many of the patterns to be compatible with precut 5" x 5" charm packs. Not only does using a charm pack save you time when coordinating prints and colors, it also allows you to achieve a scrappy look without the need for an enormous scrap stash or fabric purchase. Several projects, such as the Sew Organized Clutch on page 11 and the Live Simply Pillow on page 42, also include a bit of hand embroidery that adds a sweet handmade touch without a huge investment of time.

Every month, I meet with a group of sewing friends to make a small project together, so I love designing patterns that are short and simple enough that we can complete them in an afternoon. I hope you'll get that same feeling of fun and satisfaction from making—and especially finishing—these projects for yourself, your loved ones, and your home.

Happy sewing!

~Sherri

Cottage Charm Table Runner

Sew a sweet table runner from three simple Honeybee blocks set on point. The appliqué shapes represent the bee bodies and wings and are so easy to fuse in place.

FINISHED SIZE: 17" x 51"

Materials

Yardage is based on 42"-wide fabric unless otherwise noted.

24 squares, 5" x 5", of assorted light prints for blocks

12 squares, 5" x 5", of assorted yellow prints for blocks

4 squares, 5" x 5", of assorted mint-green prints for blocks

4 squares, 5" x 5", of assorted coral prints for setting-triangle accents

3 squares, 5" x 5", of assorted pink prints for blocks

⅝ yard of mint-green floral for setting triangles

1 fat quarter (18" x 21") of coral gingham for appliqué

⅜ yard of coral print for binding

1⅔ yards of fabric for backing

22" x 56" piece of batting

12" x 24" piece of fusible web

Cutting

All measurements include ¼" seam allowances.

From the light squares, cut:
24 squares, 3½" x 3½"

From the mint-green squares, cut:
15 squares, 2½" x 2½"

From the pink squares, cut:
12 squares, 2½" x 2½"

From the yellow squares, cut:
12 squares, 3½" x 3½"

From the coral squares, cut:
4 squares, 3½" x 3½"

From the mint-green floral, cut:
1 square, 18" x 18"; cut the square into quarters diagonally to yield 4 triangles

From the coral print for binding, cut:
4 strips, 2½" x 42"

Assembling the Blocks

1. Lay out five green 2½" squares and four pink 2½" squares in three rows of three as shown. Join the squares in each row; press the seam allowances toward the green squares. Join the rows; press the seam allowances in one direction. Make three nine-patch units, 6½" square.

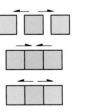

Make 3.

COTTAGE CHARM TABLE RUNNER

2. Sew together two light 3½" squares; press the seam allowances in one direction. Make 12.

Make 12.

3. Sew light-square units to the top and bottom of each nine-patch unit. Press the seam allowances toward the light squares. The units should be 6½" x 12½".

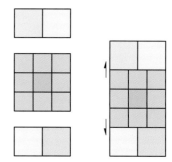

4. Sew yellow 3½" squares to the sides of the remaining six light-square units. Press the seam allowances toward the yellow squares. The units should be 3½" x 12½".

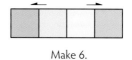

Make 6.

5. Sew the yellow-corner units to the sides of one nine-patch unit; press the seam allowances toward the yellow-corner units. Make three blocks, 12½" square.

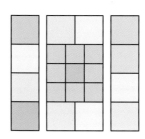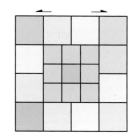

Make 3.

Assembling the Table-Runner Top

1. Draw a diagonal line from corner to corner on the wrong side of the coral 3½" squares. Place one marked square right sides together on the right-angle corner of one setting triangle as shown. Sew along the marked line. Trim the seam allowances to ¼", and then press toward the coral corner. Make four.

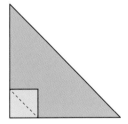 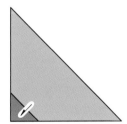

Make 4.

2. Arrange the three blocks on point, and then place the setting triangles along the edges, positioning the coral points in the center.

3. Join the blocks and triangles in diagonal rows as shown at right, pressing the seam allowances in opposite directions from row to row. Join the rows; press the seam allowances in one direction.

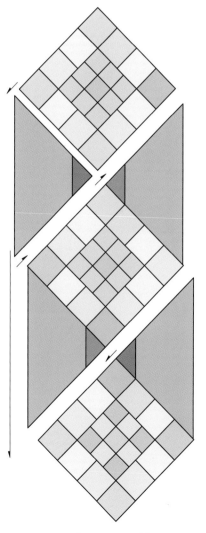

Runner assembly

Finishing the Table Runner

1. Layer the backing, batting, and table-runner top. Baste the layers together. Hand or machine quilt as desired. The table runner shown was quilted with feathers and an orange-peel pattern to highlight the various sections of the design. Trim the backing and batting even with the table-runner edges.

2. Use the coral 2½"-wide strips to make the binding. Bind the table runner according to your preferred method, or try the technique described in "Timesaving Binding" below.

Timesaving Binding

If you're in a hurry, rather than hand stitching the binding to the back of the table runner, try machine stitching it to the front instead. Fold the prepared binding strip in half with wrong sides together; press. Place the binding on the back of the table runner, aligning the raw edges of the binding and the runner. Stitch the binding in place, mitering each corner and finishing the raw ends as usual. Wrap the binding to the front of the runner, enclosing the raw edges. From the front of the runner, topstitch by machine, sewing very close to the binding fold through all layers.

Adding the Appliqué

1. Using the pattern below, trace 36 shapes onto the paper side of the fusible web. Follow the manufacturer's instructions to fuse the shapes to the wrong side of the coral-gingham fat quarter. Cut out the shapes along the drawn lines and remove the paper backing.

2. Arrange the appliqués on the table runner, referring to the photo on page 8 for placement. Fuse the pieces in place. Sew around the edges of each shape using a blanket stitch—by hand or machine.

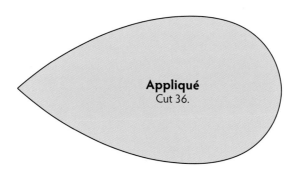

Appliqué
Cut 36.

Sew Organized Clutch

Keep supplies for portable projects organized and close at hand with a storage clutch. Make one for yourself and a few more for all of your sewing buddies!

FINISHED SIZE: 5" x 8" closed; 8" x 10" open

. . . .

Materials

Yardage is based on 42"-wide fabric unless otherwise noted.

1 fat quarter (18" x 21") of plaid for clutch

⅜ yard of cream-on-red print for accent, binding, and closure tab

10" x 12" rectangle of heavyweight interfacing (such as Timtex)

8" x 10" rectangle of lightweight fusible interfacing

8" x 10" rectangle of clear vinyl

Light-red embroidery floss

Hand-embroidery needle

2 all-purpose polyester zippers, at least 9" long

¾" x 1" rectangle of Velcro

Basting spray

Cutting

All measurements include ¼" seam allowances.

From the plaid, cut:
2 rectangles, 5½" x 8½"
1 rectangle, 8½" x 10½"

From the red print, cut:
5 strips, 1½" x 8½"
1 rectangle, 2" x 5"
2¼"-wide bias strips to yield a total length of 42"

From the vinyl, cut:
2 rectangles, 3½" x 8½"

Stitching the Embroidery

1. Using your favorite transfer method, trace the embroidery design on page 15 onto the right side of a large plaid rectangle, centered and 3" up from one of the long edges.

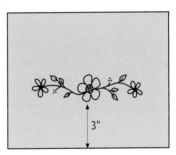

2. Fuse the rectangle of lightweight fusible interfacing to the wrong side of the marked rectangle, following the manufacturer's instructions. Using three strands of floss and referring to the embroidery key on page 15, stitch the design. Go to ShopMartingale.com/HowtoQuilt to find instructions for common hand-embroidery stitches. Press the fabric after you complete the embroidery.

3. Trim the embroidered rectangle to 5½" x 8½", keeping the embroidery centered and 1" up from one 8½" edge.

SEW THIS AND THAT!

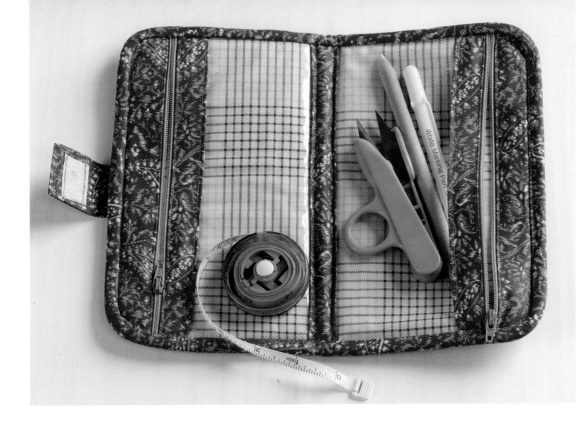

Assembling the Pockets and Closure Tab

1. With wrong sides together, fold the long edges of one red 1½" x 8½" strip to meet in the center; press. Repeat to make three double-folded strips. Fold one long edge of one remaining 1½" x 8½" strip ¼" toward the wrong side; press. Make two single-folded strips.

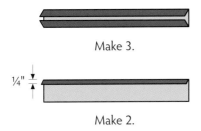

Make 3.

¼"

Make 2.

2. With the right sides facing up, center one double-folded strip along one side of one zipper tape, placing the fold ⅛" from the zipper teeth. Topstitch close to the folded edge of the strip through both layers. Place one single-folded strip right side up along the opposite side of the zipper tape, placing the fold ⅛"from the teeth. Topstitch close to the folded edge through both layers. Repeat

Vinyl Pointers

- Clear vinyl is available by the yard at most general crafting and sewing stores. If you prefer not to use vinyl, substitute coordinating fabric instead. It will look just as cute!

- Never iron directly on vinyl, as the heat will melt it and make a big mess. If you need to flatten it a bit, place a heavy dish towel over the vinyl and press quickly. Wait until *after* pressing to cut out the pieces, because heat can cause vinyl to shrink slightly.

- If the vinyl sticks to the sewing-machine bed as you sew, cut a piece of tissue paper the same size as the vinyl piece. Layer the tissue paper under the vinyl during sewing, and then simply rip it away. Use a slightly shorter stitch length so you don't pull out the stitches along with the tissue.

to sew one double-folded and one single-folded strip to the remaining zipper. Trim the zipper ends even with the fabric strips, trimming away the lower zipper stop and upper tape ends as needed.

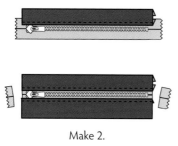

Make 2.

3. Place the free long edge of one double-folded fabric strip ⅜" over one long edge of a 3½" x 8½" vinyl rectangle. Topstitch the fold through both layers. Repeat to make two vinyl pockets.

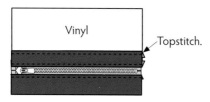

Make 2.

4. Fold the red 2" x 5" rectangle in half widthwise; press to mark the center. Unfold the rectangle, and then place one side of the Velcro ½" from the center fold on the right side of the fabric. Sew around the perimeter of the Velcro through both layers. With right sides together, fold the rectangle along the original fold line. Sew both long sides. Turn the rectangle right side out; press flat. Topstitch the sides and top to complete the closure tab.

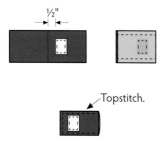

Assembling the Clutch

1. Place the two plaid 5½" x 8½" rectangles right sides together, orienting the embroidery along the lower edge. Sew the lower edges together, and then press open to make the 8½" x 10½" outer panel.

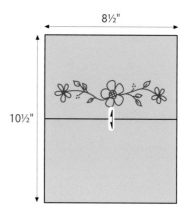

2. Center the remaining side of the Velcro ¾" down from the top edge of the outer panel. Stitch around the perimeter of the Velcro piece. Center the closure tab with the Velcro side up along the bottom edge of the outer panel as shown. Baste the edge of the tab to the panel using a ⅛" seam allowance.

3. Spray the wrong sides of the outer panel and the remaining plaid 8½" x 10½" rectangle (inner panel) with basting spray. Sandwich the heavyweight interfacing between the panels, finger-pressing lightly to adhere.

4. Place the clutch with the inner panel facing up. Position the pockets over the inner panel, orienting the zippers toward the outer edges; pin in place. The vinyl edges may overlap slightly at the center. Place the remaining double-folded strip over the center where the vinyl edges meet; pin. Stitch the long edges of the double-folded strip through all layers.

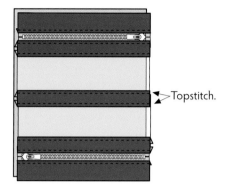

Topstitch.

5. Round the corners of the clutch by tracing the edge of a spool of thread and then cutting away the excess.

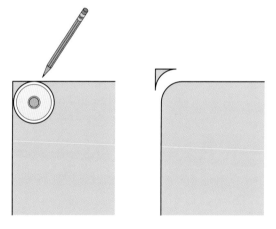

Finishing the Clutch

To make the binding, join the red bias strips at a 45° angle; press the seam allowances open. Bind according to your preferred method, or refer to "Timesaving Binding" on page 10. Ease the binding around the curved corners and sew carefully over the zipper ends. This method of machine stitching the binding first to the inside of the clutch prevents you from having to hand stitch the binding to the vinyl.

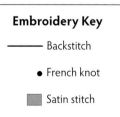

Embroidery Key	
——	Backstitch
●	French knot
▧	Satin stitch

Bird-Watching Pillow

Embroider a fine feathered friend onto a colorful patchwork pillow. Use coordinating precut charm squares or scraps from your stash to give the pillow an eclectic look.

FINISHED SIZE: 16" x 16"

. . . .

Materials

Yardage is based on 42"-wide fabric unless otherwise noted.

12 squares, 5" x 5", of assorted red, blue, yellow, and green prints for pillow-front patchwork

2 squares, 5" x 5", of navy print for corner triangles

1 fat quarter (18" x 21") of tan solid for embroidery background

½ yard of red print for backing

15" x 15" square of lightweight fusible interfacing

16" x 16" pillow form

Embroidery floss in brown, red, green, gold, and blue

4 assorted buttons, ⅞" diameter

Hand-embroidery needle

Cutting

All measurements include ¼" seam allowances.

From the tan solid, cut:
1 square, 15" x 15"

From the assorted print squares, cut:
24 rectangles, 2½" x 4½"

From the navy squares, cut:
4 squares, 2½" x 2½"

From the red print for backing, cut:
2 rectangles, 16½" x 20"

Stitching the Embroidery

1. Using your favorite transfer method, center and trace the embroidery design on page 19 onto the right side of the tan background square.

2. Fuse the interfacing square to the wrong side of the background square, following the manufacturer's instructions. Using three strands of floss and referring to the embroidery key on page 19, stitch the design. You'll find instructions for some common hand-embroidery stitches at ShopMartingale.com/HowtoQuilt. Press the fabric when the embroidery is complete.

3. Trim the tan square to 8½" x 8½", keeping the embroidery centered.

4. Draw a diagonal line from corner to corner on the wrong side of the navy squares. Place the marked squares on the corners of the tan square with right sides together,

orienting the drawn lines as shown. Sew over the drawn lines, and then trim the seam allowances to ¼". Press toward the navy corners.

Assembling the Pillow

1. Sew two print 2½" x 4½" rectangles together along the short edges; press the seam allowances toward the darker fabric. Make two units, 8½" long. Sew three print 2½" x 4½" rectangles together along the short edges; press the seam allowances in one direction. Make four units, 12½" long. Sew four print 2½" x 4½" rectangles together along the short edges; press the seam allowances in one direction. Make two units, 16½" long.

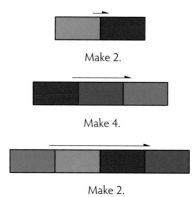

Make 2.

Make 4.

Make 2.

2. Sew the 8½" units to the sides of the tan square; press the seam allowances toward the units. Sew 12½" units to the top and bottom of the tan square; press. Sew the remaining 12½" units to the sides of the pillow front; press. Sew the 16½" units to the top and bottom of the pillow front; press. The front should be 16½" square.

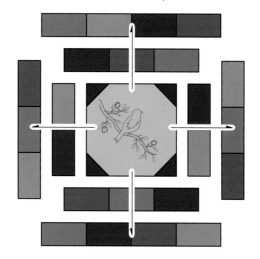

3. Hand sew buttons to the corners of the tan square.

4. Fold each backing rectangle in half widthwise, making two 10" x 16½" rectangles. Place the pillow front right side up, and then place the backing rectangles over the pillow front, matching the raw edges and overlapping the long folded edges of the rectangles; pin. Stitch around the perimeter of the layers. Clip the corners.

5. Turn the pillow cover right side out through the back opening; press. Insert the pillow form into the cover.

Embroidery Key

---------- Stem stitch

● French knot

Button Bliss Pouch

Stitch a colorful button-embellished pouch that's ideal for storing makeup or small sewing supplies. The handy strap allows the bag to double as a cute wristlet.

FINISHED SIZE: 9" x 6"

Materials

Yardage is based on 42"-wide fabric unless otherwise noted.

11 squares, 5" x 5", of assorted bright prints for outer pouch
1 fat eighth (9" x 21") of green print for front accent and strap
¼ yard of yellow print for lining
¼ yard of heavyweight fusible interfacing
12"-long all-purpose polyester zipper
5 assorted bright buttons, ¾" to 1⅛" diameter

Cutting

All measurements include ¼" seam allowances.

From the bright squares, cut:
42 squares, 2" x 2"

From the green print, cut:
1 strip, 2" x 9½"
1 strip, 2¼" x 12"
2 squares, 1¼" x 1¼"

From the yellow print, cut:
2 rectangles, 6½" x 9½"

From the interfacing, cut:
2 rectangles, 6½" x 9½"

Preparing the Pouch Pieces

1. Sew six bright squares together into a row. Press the seam allowances in one direction. Make seven rows, 2" x 9½".

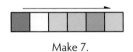

Make 7.

2. Lay out three rows of squares and the green 2" x 9½" strip as shown. Sew together along the long edges to make the front of the pouch. Hand sew the buttons to the green strip, referring to the photo on page 21 for placement. Press the seam allowances toward the green strip. Sew the remaining four rows together to make the back of the pouch. The pouch front and back should each be 6½" x 9½".

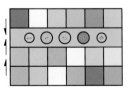

Front

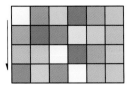

Back

BUTTON BLISS POUCH

3. Fuse the interfacing rectangles to the wrong sides of the front and back pieces.

4. Trace the template on page 23, including the lines for the dart, onto the lower corners of the bag front and back and the wrong side of the yellow 6½" x 9½" lining rectangles. Trim away the excess fabric, but don't trim into the dart. Fold each piece right sides together along the dart and match the lines of one dart. Sew along the line, backstitching at the dart point. Press the dart to one side. Repeat to sew a dart in each lower corner of the outer panels and lining pieces.

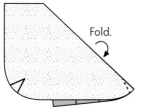 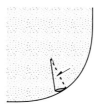

Fold.

5. Fold the long edges of the green 2¼" x 12" strip with wrong sides together to meet at the center; press. Fold the strip in half lengthwise, enclosing the raw edges; press. Topstitch the long edges of the strip. Then fold the strip in half widthwise and place the strip on the right side of the front panel, 1" from the top edge, aligning the raw edges; baste.

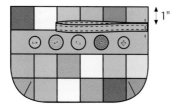

1"

6. Fold each green 1¼" square in half; press. Place a square on the top end of the zipper, moving the zipper pull just below the fold. Topstitch the fold. Measure 9½" from the top end of the zipper and place the remaining folded square across the zipper at that point. Sew in place, stitching carefully over the zipper teeth. Trim the excess zipper.

Assembling the Pouch

1. Place the zipper along the top edge of the front panel with right sides together. Baste the zipper tape to the panel using a ⅛" seam allowance.

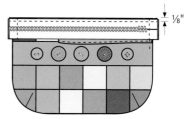

⅛"

2. Place one lining piece right side down over the front panel, sandwiching the zipper. Using a zipper sewing-machine foot, sew the top edge close to the zipper teeth.

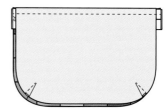

3. Fold the front panel and lining away from the zipper; press. Topstitch the pouch top edge. Repeat the process in step 2 to sew the back panel and remaining lining piece to the opposite side of the zipper, and then topstitch the top edge.

4. Unzip the zipper halfway. Fold the lining pieces away from the front and back panels and place them right sides together. Match the front and back panels with right sides together; pin generously. Sew around the perimeter of the lining and outer pieces, leaving a 3" opening in the lining for turning.

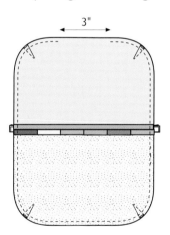

3"

Strong Stitching

Be sure to backstitch securely at both ends of the opening in the pouch lining to prevent the stitching from popping when you turn the pouch right side out.

5. Turn the bag right side out through the opening in the lining. Hand or machine sew the opening closed. Push the lining into the bag; press thoroughly.

Corner template

Spring Garden Table Runner

Bring the beauty of the garden to your dining table with a charming runner. The pattern is designed for 5" squares, so you can save time by using precut charm packs.

FINISHED SIZE: 15½" x 33½"

Materials

Yardage is based on 42"-wide fabric unless otherwise noted.

29 squares, 5" x 5", of assorted pink, aqua, coral, and yellow prints for blocks and border

21 squares, 5" x 5", of white solid for background

13 squares, 5" x 5", of assorted coral prints for blocks

¼ yard of coral gingham for binding

⅝ yard of fabric for backing

22" x 41" piece of batting

Cutting

All measurements include ¼" seam allowances.

From 3 of the coral squares, cut:
12 squares, 2⅜" x 2⅜"

From 6 of the coral squares, cut:
24 squares, 2" x 2"

From 1 aqua and 2 yellow squares, cut:
3 squares, 3½" x 3½"

From 4 of the coral squares, cut:
4 squares, 3½" x 3½"

From 26 of the pink, aqua, and yellow squares, cut:
48 rectangles, 2" x 3½"

From 12 of the white squares, cut:
24 rectangles, 2" x 3½"

From 6 of the white squares, cut:
24 squares, 2" x 2"

From 3 of the white squares, cut:
12 squares, 2⅜" x 2⅜"

From the coral gingham, cut:
3 strips, 2½" x 42"

Assembling the Blocks

1. Draw a diagonal line from corner to corner on the wrong side of the white 2⅜" squares. Place a marked square right sides together with a coral 2⅜" square. Sew ¼" from each side of the drawn line. Cut along the line to yield two half-square-triangle units. Press the seam allowances toward the coral triangles. Make 24.

Make 24.

SPRING GARDEN TABLE RUNNER

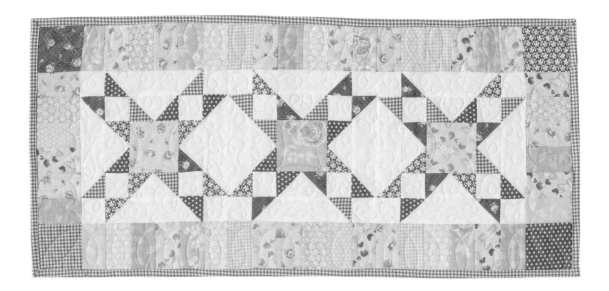

2. Draw a diagonal line from corner to corner on the wrong side of the coral 2" squares. Place a marked square on one end of a white 2" x 3½" rectangle with right sides together as shown. Sew along the line, and then trim the seam allowances to ¼". Press toward the coral corner. Repeat to sew a second print square to the opposite end of the rectangle. Make 12 star-point units, 2" x 3½".

Make 12.

3. Sew a white 2" square to each end of six star-point units. Press the seam allowances toward the squares. The units should be 2" x 6½".

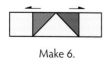

Make 6.

4. Stitch the remaining six star-point units to the sides of the yellow and aqua 3½" squares. Press the seam allowances toward the squares. The units should be 3½" x 6½".

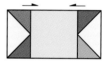

Make 3.

5. Sew units from step 3 to each of the units from step 4 as shown to make three stars, 6½" square. Press.

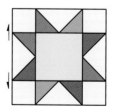

Make 3.

6. Stitch half-square-triangle units to the ends of a white 2" x 3½" rectangle. Press the seam allowances toward the rectangle. Make 12 units, 2" x 6½".

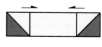

Make 12.

SEW THIS AND THAT!

7. Stitch white 2" squares to to the ends of six units from step 6. Press as shown. The units should be 2" x 9½".

Make 6.

8. Sew units from step 6 to the sides of the star unit. Press the seam allowances toward the star unit. Sew units from step 7 to the top and bottom of the star unit. Press as shown. Make three blocks, 9½" square.

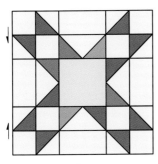

Make 3.

9. Sew the three blocks together into a row, placing the aqua-square block in the center. Press the seam allowances in one direction.

Assembling the Table-Runner Top

1. Join 18 print 2" x 3½" rectangles along the long edges; press the seam allowances in one direction. Make two units, 3½" x 27½".

Make 2.

2. Sew two coral 3½" squares and six print rectangles together as shown; press the seam allowances in one direction. Make two units, 3½" x 15½".

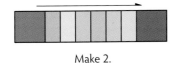

Make 2.

3. Sew the long border strips to the sides of the table-runner center; press the seam allowances toward the borders. Sew the short border strips to the ends; press.

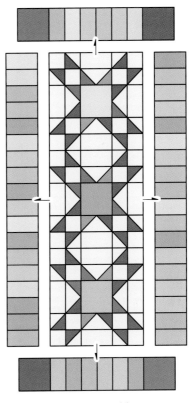

Runner assembly

Finishing the Table Runner

1. Layer the backing, batting, and table-runner top. Baste the layers together. Hand or machine quilt as desired. The table runner shown was quilted with a swirl-and-loop pattern in the background and a loop design in the border.

2. Use the coral 2½"-wide strips to make the binding. Bind the table runner according to your preferred method, or refer to "Timesaving Binding" on page 10.

Daisy Delight Candle Mat

A quick and easy mat makes a charming setting for a candle. Embroider the corners with a quartet of dancing daisies.

FINISHED SIZE: 16" x 16"

Materials

Yardage is based on 42"-wide fabric unless otherwise noted.

¼ yard of yellow floral for outer border

1 fat quarter (18" x 21") of white-on-white print for background

1 fat eighth (9" x 21") of pink tone on tone for inner border

1 fat quarter of fabric for backing

18" x 18" square of lightweight fusible interfacing

18" x 18" square of lightweight batting

Embroidery floss in yellow, pink, dark pink, and mossy green

Hand-embroidery needle

Cutting

All measurements include ¼" seam allowances.

From the pink tone on tone, cut:
8 strips, 1" x 9"

From the yellow floral, cut:
8 strips, 2½" x 11"

From the backing fat quarter, cut:
1 square, 18" x 18"

Stitching the Embroidery

1. Draw an 11½" square on the right side of the white fat quarter. Be sure to draw a precise, accurate square; the fabric will be trimmed to this size after embroidery. Mark each side of the square 2¼" from each corner. Draw a diagonal line connecting the marks at each corner.

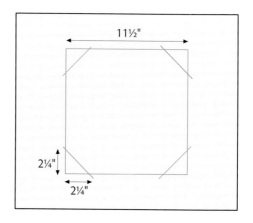

2. Using your favorite transfer method, trace the embroidery design on page 31 onto each corner of the square within the diagonal lines, referring to the photo on page 30 for placement.

3. Center the fusible interfacing behind the drawn square on the wrong side of the fabric; fuse following the manufacturer's instructions. Using three strands of floss and referring to the key that accompanies the embroidery pattern, stitch the design. Go to ShopMartingale.com/HowtoQuilt for instructions on common hand-embroidery stitches. Press the fabric after you complete the embroidery, and then trim to 11½" square. Trim away the corners beyond each diagonal line to create an octagon.

DAISY DELIGHT CANDLE MAT

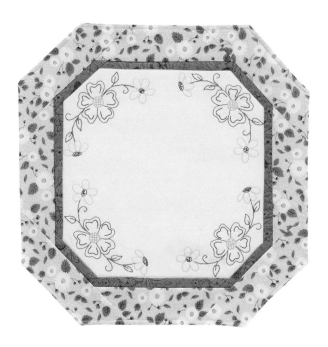

Assembling the Candle Mat

1. With right sides together, position a pink 1" x 9" strip on the top, bottom, and sides of the mat. Stitch the strips to the edges; press them away from the center. Trim away the excess strip fabric even with the mat edges. Repeat to stitch the remaining pink strips to the remaining four edges; press.

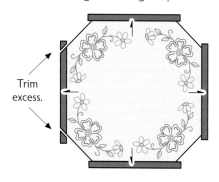

Trim excess.

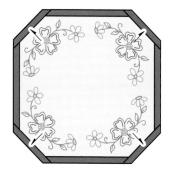

2. Repeat step 1 to sew the yellow 2½" x 11" strips to the edges of the mat. Press the strips away from the center.

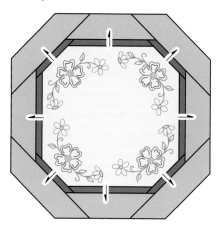

3. Place the backing fabric right side up over the batting. Press to add a bit of static cling to hold the layers together. Center the candle mat over the backing fabric with right sides together. Sew around the perimeter of the mat, leaving a 3" opening on one side.

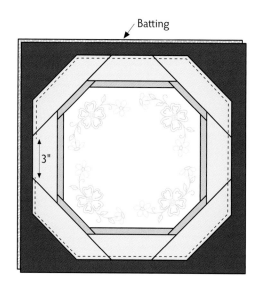

Batting

3"

4. Trim the excess batting and backing fabric even with the edges of the mat. Clip the corners to reduce bulk.

5. Turn the candle mat right side out through the opening; press thoroughly. Hand stitch the opening closed.

6. Quilt the mat as desired. The mat shown was quilted around the outer edges and in the ditch along the seams to add dimension.

Choosing Colors

The embroidery-floss colors complement the shades of pink, yellow, and green in the floral print. You can coordinate colors in the same way by matching floss to your outer-border print.

Embroidery Key	
——	Backstitch
●	French knot

Making Memories Journal Cover

Dress up an everyday composition book with an adorable fabric cover. This fast and fun project makes a wonderful gift for the list-makers and note-takers in your life.

FINISHED SIZE: 7⅝" x 9⅞"

. . . .

Materials

12 squares, 5" x 5", of assorted bright red, pink, blue, and green prints for patchwork

1 fat quarter (18" x 21") of aqua gingham for center strip

1 fat quarter of aqua floral for inner flaps and ties

Scraps of coordinating bright pink, red, and green prints for appliqué

1 sheet, 9" x 12", of fusible web

Standard-size (7½" x 9¾") composition book

Cutting

All measurements include ¼" seam allowances.

From the bright squares, cut:
12 rectangles, 3" x 3¼"

From the aqua gingham, cut:
1 rectangle, 15½" x 21"; crosscut into 1 rectangle, 10¼" x 15½", and 1 strip, 4¾" x 15½"

From the aqua floral, cut:
2 rectangles, 10¼" x 10½"
2 strips, 2" x 11½"

Making the Front Panel

1. Stitch six bright rectangles together along the 3¼" edges. Press the seam allowances in one direction. Make two strips, 3¼" x 15½".

Make 2.

2. Stitch the pieced strips to the long edges of the gingham 4¾" x 15½" strip. Press the seam allowances toward the gingham. The front panel should be 10¼" x 15½".

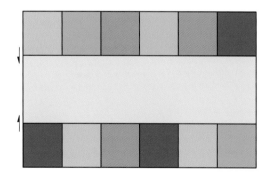

3. Using the patterns on page 35, trace the appliqué shapes onto the paper side of the fusible web. Follow the manufacturer's instructions to fuse the pieces to the wrong side of the pink, red, and green scraps. Cut out the pieces along the drawn lines.

4. Position the appliqué pieces right side up on the gingham strip, approximately 2" from the right edge. Refer to the photo on page 32 for placement. Fuse the pieces in place. Use a hand or machine blanket stitch to sew around the edges of each appliqué shape.

Assembling the Cover

1. Fold the long edges of both floral 2" x 11½" strips toward the wrong side to meet in the center; press. Fold in half again, enclosing the raw edges; press. Topstitch the long edges to make two ties.

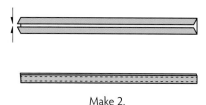

Make 2.

2. To make the inner flaps, fold each floral 10¼" x 10½" rectangle in half lengthwise with right sides together to measure 10¼" x 5¼"; press.

3. With the cover facing right side up, center the ties along the sides, matching the raw edges. Baste the tie ends in place.

4. With right sides together, place the inner flaps on the sides of the cover, aligning the raw edges.

Folded edges.

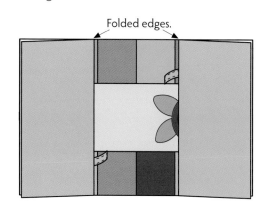

5. Place the gingham 10¼" x 15½" rectangle right side down over the cover, sandwiching the flaps. Pin the layers together around the perimeter. Stitch along the outer edges, leaving a 2½" opening on the bottom edge for turning.

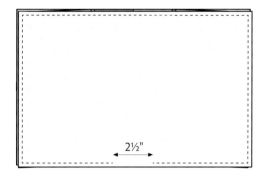

6. Clip the corners, and then turn the cover right side out; press thoroughly. Hand stitch the opening closed. Insert the front and back covers of the composition book into the flaps.

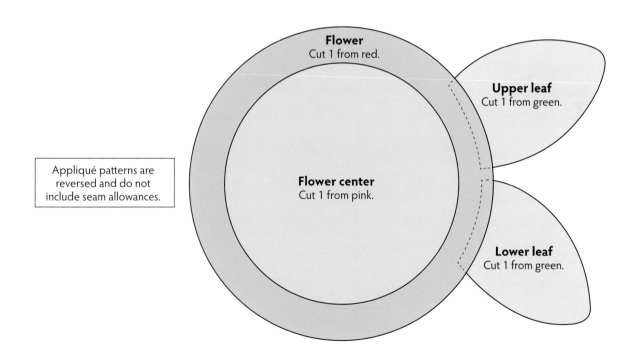

Appliqué patterns are reversed and do not include seam allowances.

Flower
Cut 1 from red.

Upper leaf
Cut 1 from green.

Flower center
Cut 1 from pink.

Lower leaf
Cut 1 from green.

All Squared Up Tote

Showcase your favorite fabric prints on the front of a handy tote bag. It's the perfect size for an outing to the quilt shop or farmers' market.

FINISHED SIZE: 16" x 13" (excluding handles)

Materials

Yardage is based on 42"-wide fabric unless otherwise noted.

1 yard of yellow gingham for outer bag and handles

20 squares, 2½" x 2½", of assorted bright prints for front accents

⅝ yard of red print for handle accents and lining

1 fat quarter (18" x 21") of blue print for inner pockets

2¾ yards of 22"-wide medium-weight fusible interfacing

2 rectangles, 2" x 8", of fusible web

20"-long all-purpose polyester zipper

Square Deal

This bag pattern is perfectly suited to using precut 2½" fabric squares, known as mini charms. If you don't have mini charms on hand, cut a scrappy selection from your fabric stash or from leftover precut 2½"-wide strips.

Cutting

All measurements include ¼" seam allowances.

From the yellow gingham, cut:
1 strip, 2½" x 42" strip; crosscut into 24 rectangles, 1½" x 2½"
1 strip, 16½" x 42"; crosscut into 1 strip, 4½" x 16½", and 2 strips, 5½" x 16½"
1 rectangle, 13½" x 20½"
5 strips, 1½" x 16½"
2 strips, 2½" x 13½"
2 strips, 4" x 18½"
1 rectangle, 2½" x 4½"

From the red print, cut:
2 strips, 2" x 18½"
2 rectangles, 13½" x 20½"

From the blue print, cut:
2 rectangles, 8½" x 20½"

From the interfacing, cut:
2 strips, 4" x 18½"
2 rectangles, 8½" x 20½"
4 rectangles, 13½" x 20½"
1 rectangle, 4½" x 16½"
2 strips, 5½" x 16½"

ALL SQUARED UP TOTE

Press the seam allowances toward the strips. The panel should be 13½" x 20½".

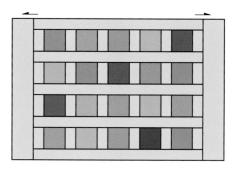

Assembling the Outer Bag

1. Fuse the corresponding interfacing pieces to the wrong sides of the pieced bag front, yellow 13½" x 20½" rectangle, yellow 4½" x 16½" rectangle, blue 8½" x 20½" rectangles, and red 13½" x 20½" rectangles.

2. Center the yellow 4½" x 16½" rectangle along the bottom edge of the bag front with right sides together. Sew the rectangle to the bag front; press. Sew the opposite edge of the rectangle to one long edge of the yellow 13½" x 20½" rectangle; press.

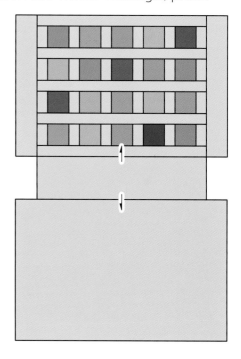

Assembling the Bag Front

1. Arrange six yellow 1½" x 2½" rectangles alternating with five bright 2½" squares to form a row. Sew the rectangles and squares together; press the seam allowances in one direction. Make four rows, 2½" x 16½".

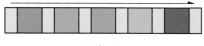

Make 4.

2. Lay out the four pieced rows alternating with five yellow 1½" x 16½" strips. Sew the strips and rows together; press the seam allowances toward the strips. Sew a yellow 2½" x 13½" strip to each side of the panel.

3. Fold the bag in half, right sides together, matching the sides and corners. Sew the sides of the bag; press the seam allowances open. Match the side seams and center of the bottom piece; box the lower corners by sewing across the openings.

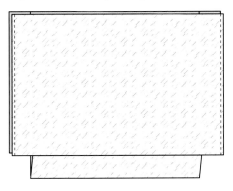

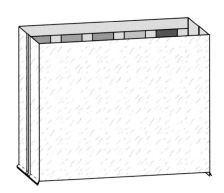

Assembling the Lining

1. Cut a 2¼" square from each bottom corner of the red 13½" x 20½" rectangles. Center one 2" x 8" rectangle of fusible web within each lower section of the red lining pieces on the wrong sides. Fuse the rectangles in place, but don't remove the paper backing.

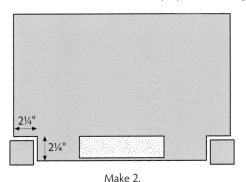

Make 2.

2. To make the inner pockets, fold each blue 8½" x 20½" rectangle in half lengthwise with right sides together. Sew the sides of the pockets, and then turn them right side out; press. Fold the unfinished edges ¼" toward the wrong side; press.

3. Center one pocket on the right side of each red lining piece, 3½" up from the bottom edge. Stitch the sides and bottom edge of each pocket, leaving the upper edge open.

4. Place the lining pieces right sides together. Stitch the sides, and then stitch the bottom edge, leaving a centered 3" opening.

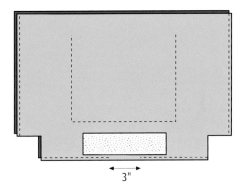

5. Box the bottom corners of the lining in the same manner as for the outer bag.

Assembling the Zipper

1. Fuse the corresponding interfacing pieces to the wrong sides of the yellow 5½" x 16½" strips. Fold the short ends of each strip ½" toward the wrong side; press. Fold the long edges ½" toward the wrong side; press. Fold the strips in half lengthwise with wrong sides together, enclosing all of the raw edges; press.

2. Insert one zipper-tape edge into the long open edge of one of the strips. The folded edge of the strip should be about ⅛" from the zipper teeth, and the upper edge of the zipper tape should be aligned with one

short end of the strip. Topstitch the strip open edge through all layers. Repeat to stitch the remaining strip to the opposite zipper tape. Trim the top of the zipper tape even with the strips, but don't trim away the zipper teeth stops.

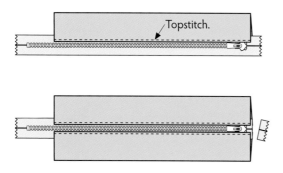

3. Fold all edges of the yellow 2½" x 4½" rectangle ½" toward the wrong side; press. Fold the rectangle in half widthwise to create a 1½" square; press. Place the end of the zipper inside of the folded square, and then sew around the perimeter of the square. Stitch carefully over the zipper teeth.

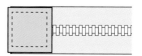

Assembling the Handles

1. Fuse the corresponding interfacing strips to the wrong sides of the two yellow 4" x 18½" strips. Fold the long edges of the strips toward the wrong side to meet in the center; press.

2. Fold the long edges of each red 2" x 18½" strip toward the wrong side to meet in the center; press.

3. Center one red strip over one yellow strip, with wrong sides together and concealing the raw edges; pin in place. Topstitch the long edges of the red strip. Make two handles.

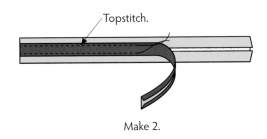

Topstitch.

Make 2.

Topstitching Tip

To give your topstitching a polished, professional look, select a slightly longer than normal stitch length. Longer stitches lie more smoothly and make it easier to achieve a straight, even line. Install an edgestitching presser foot or one with marked guidelines to make it easy to stitch parallel to the fabric edge.

Finishing the Bag

1. Keep the outer bag turned wrong side out. With right sides together, pin the ends of one handle to the top edge of the front of the bag, 4" from the side seams. Make sure the red strip will be facing outward and that the strap isn't twisted. Repeat to pin the remaining handle to the bag back.

2. Unzip the zipper entirely. With right sides together, center the fabric edges of each zipper strip along the top edges of the front and back of the bag. Pin or baste the strips in place.

3. Place the lining inside of the outer bag with right sides together, aligning the top edges and side seams; pin generously. Sew the top edges together, catching the zipper strips and handle ends.

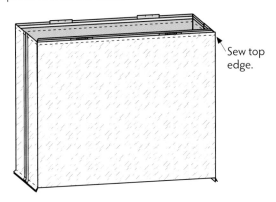

Sew top edge.

4. Remove the fusible-web paper and turn the bag right side out through the opening in the lining. Push the lining and zipper strip into the bag. Press thoroughly so that the lining is fused to the bag to secure it. Topstitch the top edge of the bag.

5. Press the bottom of the bag to secure the fusible web on the lining to the outer-bag fabric. Hand stitch the opening closed.

Live Simply Pillow

Use a fun and easy string-piecing technique to make a colorful throw pillow. Embroider pretty flowers and a personalized message for a one-of-a-kind pillow.

FINISHED SIZE: 18" x 18"

. . . .

Materials

Yardage is based on 42"-wide fabric unless otherwise noted.

⅛ yard *each* of 6 to 8 assorted bright prints for strip piecing

1 fat quarter (18" x 21") of cream print for embroidery background

⅜ yard of muslin for strip-piecing foundation

⅝ yard of fabric for backing

18" x 21" rectangle of lightweight fusible interfacing

18" x 18" pillow form

Embroidery floss in yellow, red, light green, medium green, coral, and aqua

Hand-embroidery needle

1 pink-and-yellow button, 1¼" diameter

Cutting

All measurements include ¼" seam allowances.

From the bright prints, cut:
Approximately 36 strips, 2" x 13"*

From the muslin, cut:
4 squares, 10" x 10"

From the backing fabric, cut:
1 square, 18½" x 18½"

*The total number of strips you need depends on how wide or narrow you choose to make the angled stripes on the pillow.

Stitching the Embroidery

1. On the right side of the cream fat quarter, draw four rectangles measuring 3" x 14½". Using your preferred transfer method, trace the flower embroidery design on page 45 onto the center of three rectangles. Trace the "Live Simply" lettering onto the center of one rectangle.

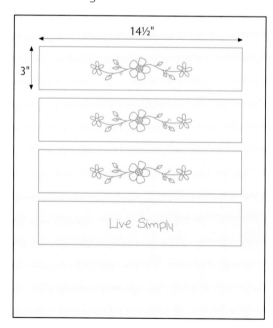

2. Fuse the interfacing rectangle to the wrong side of the cream fat quarter. Using three strands of floss and referring to the embroidery key on page 45, stitch the

LIVE SIMPLY PILLOW

designs. You can find instructions for common hand-embroidery stitches at ShopMartingale.com/HowtoQuilt. Press the fabric after you complete the embroidery.

3. Cut out the four 3" x 14½" rectangles.

Assembling the Blocks

1. Place the muslin square on a flat work surface. Place one of the embroidered rectangles right side up across the diagonal center of the muslin square as shown. Place a bright print strip right side down over the embroidered strip at a slightly wonky angle. Sew the edge of the bright strip through all layers. Press the bright strip away from the embroidered strip.

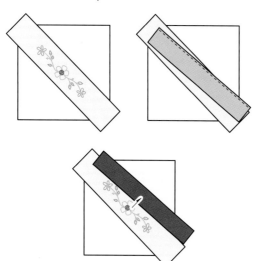

2. Continue adding bright strips to the muslin square in the same manner until all of the muslin is covered. For the smaller corner areas of the squares, you can save fabric by using scraps from previous strips if desired. Trim the block to 9½" square, making sure to keep the embroidery centered. Make four blocks.

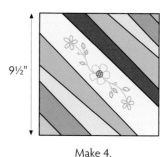

Make 4.

Assembling the Pillow

1. Arrange the blocks in two rows, positioning the strips to form a diamond pattern as shown in the photo on page 43. Join the blocks in each row; press the seam allowances in opposite directions. Join the rows; press the seam allowances in one direction.

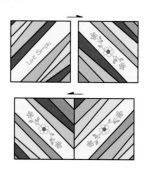

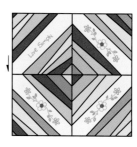

In the Mix

Take an improvisational approach when you're sewing the print strips to the muslin foundation. Aim for a pleasing distribution of colors, but don't worry too much about placing them perfectly. The slightly random, eclectic look of the various strip widths, colors, and angles adds to the charm!

2. Place the pillow front and backing square with right sides together. Sew around the perimeter, leaving an 8" opening on one side for turning.

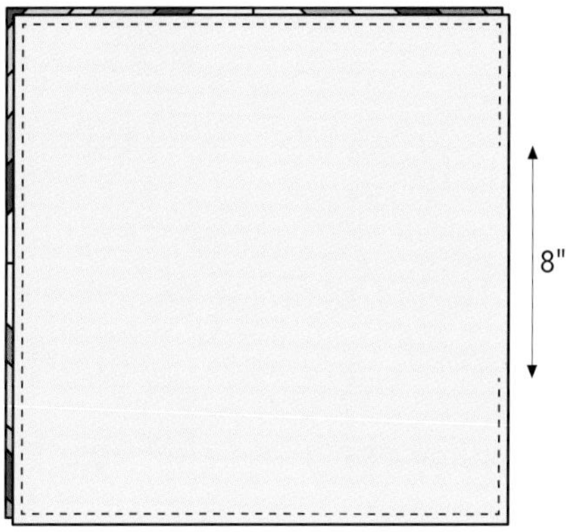

3. Clip the corners, and then turn the pillow cover right side out; press. Insert the pillow form into the cover. Hand stitch the opening closed. Hand stitch the button to the center of the pillow through all of the layers for a tufted effect.

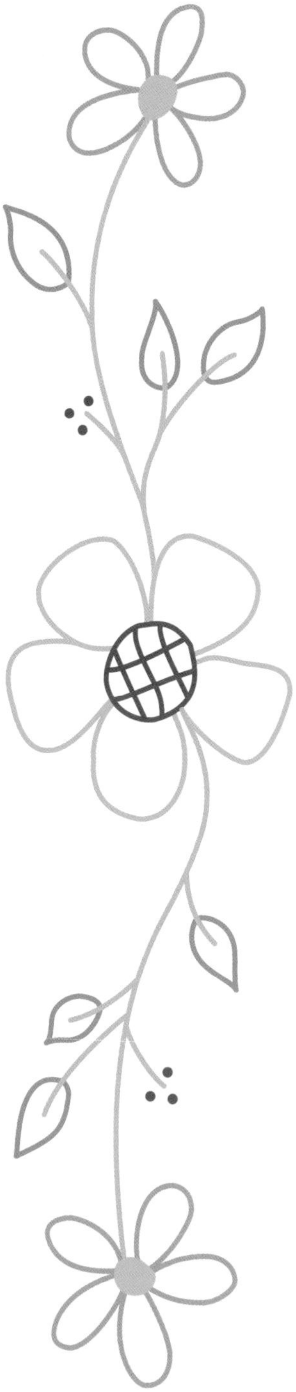

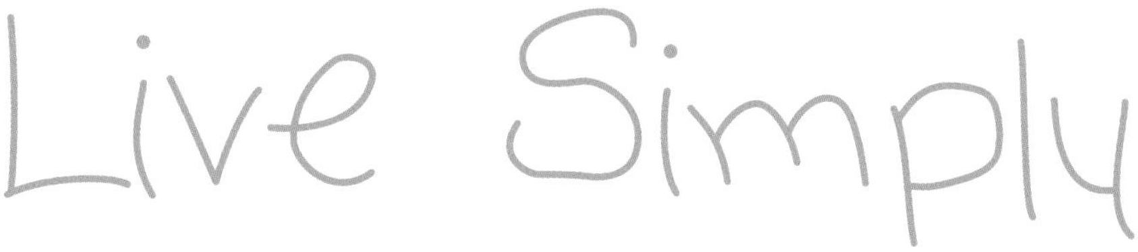

Embroidery Key

- Backstitch
- French knot
- Satin stitch

Confetti Table Runner

Set the table in style with a quick-to-make runner. The lattice-like pattern looks lovely from every angle.

FINISHED SIZE: 17" x 42"

Materials

Yardage is based on 42"-wide fabric unless otherwise noted.

⅛ yard *each* of 4 light prints for background

19 squares, 5" x 5", *total* of bright orange, green, red, pink, and blue prints for blocks

1 fat quarter (18" x 21") of green print for setting triangles

¼ yard of red polka dot for binding

1½ yards of fabric for backing

22" x 47" piece of batting

Cutting

All measurements include ¼" seam allowances.

From the light prints, cut:
26 rectangles, 1½" x 4½"
26 rectangles, 1½" x 6½"

From *6* of the bright squares, cut:
52 squares, 1½" x 1½"

From *13* of the bright squares, cut:
26 rectangles, 1½" x 2½"
26 rectangles, 1½" x 4½"

From the green print, cut:
2 squares, 9¾" x 9¾"; cut the squares into quarters diagonally to yield 8 triangles (2 are extra)

From the red polka dot, cut:
3 strips, 2½" x 42"

Stitched with Charm

Follow these handy tips when making a project with 5" x 5" charm squares.

- Don't prewash precut charm squares, as you'll end up with a frayed mess. If you're worried about the fabric dyes bleeding, wash the finished project with a color catcher that will soak up excess dye like a sponge.

- Precut fabrics have a pinked edge to prevent raveling. Always measure the seam allowance from the outer points of the pinked triangles to ensure accuracy.

- If your project requires additional fabric yardage, like the green print used for the setting triangles in this table runner, choose one of the prints from the same collection as your charm pack. If the same collection isn't available, stop by a local quilt shop and ask for help in finding a suitable coordinating print and color.

CONFETTI TABLE RUNNER

Assembling the Blocks

1. Arrange four bright 1½" squares in two rows. Sew the squares together in each row; press the seam allowances in opposite directions. Sew the rows together to make a four-patch unit, 2½" square. Press the seam allowances in one direction.

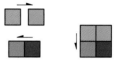

2. Sew bright 1½" x 2½" rectangles to the sides of the four-patch unit. Press the seam allowances toward the rectangles. Sew bright 1½" x 4½" rectangles to the top and bottom of the unit; press. The unit should be 4½" square.

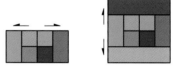

3. Sew light 1½" x 4½" rectangles to the sides of the unit. Press the seam allowances toward the light rectangles. Sew light 1½" x 6½" rectangles to the top and bottom of the unit; press. Make 13 blocks, mixing the various prints and colors for a scrappy effect. Each should be 6½" square.

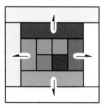

Make 13.

Assembling the Table-Runner Top

Arrange the blocks and setting triangles in five diagonal rows as shown at right. Join the blocks and triangles in each row, pressing the seam allowances in opposite directions from row to row. Join the rows; press the seam allowances in one direction.

Finishing the Table Runner

1. Layer the backing, batting, and table-runner top. Baste the layers together. Hand or machine quilt as desired. The table runner shown was quilted with a swirl-and-loop pattern in the blocks and a feather design in the setting triangles.

2. Use the red 2½"-wide strips to make the binding. Bind the table runner according to your preferred method, or refer to "Timesaving Binding" on page 10.

Runner assembly

Pickin' Sweet Tote

Stow your essentials in this simple, roomy tote decorated with a row of half-square triangles. For a unique detail, attach the shoulder straps to the tote with metal grommets.

FINISHED SIZE: 15½" x 13" x 2½" (excluding handles)

Materials

Yardage is based on 42"-wide fabric.

½ yard of navy gingham for outer bag

½ yard of white-on-red polka dot for accents and handles

⅝ yard of aqua floral for lining

⅝ yard of white print for inner pockets

9 squares, 5" x 5", of assorted green, red, navy, white, aqua, and pink prints for patchwork*

18½" x 28" rectangle of firm fusible interfacing (such as Pellon Décor-Bond)

2 yards of 1"-wide cotton webbing for handle lining

4 metal eyelets, ⁷⁄₁₆" diameter

1½" covered button kit and fabric scrap**

Feel free to incorporate more than the minimum of 9 prints for a scrappier look.

**Fussy-cut the scrap for the covered button if desired.*

Cutting

All measurements include ¼" seam allowances.

From the navy gingham, cut:
3 rectangles, 6½" x 18½"

From the white-on-red polka dot, cut:
2 strips, 4" x 33"
4 strips, 2" x 18½"
1 strip, 2½" x 42"
1 strip, 2" x 6½"

From each print 5" square, cut:
4 squares, 2½" x 2½" (36 total)

From the aqua floral, cut:
1 rectangle, 18½" x 28½"

From the white print, cut:
2 strips, 16½" x 18½"

From the cotton webbing, cut:
2 strips, 1" x 32"

Assembling the Outer Bag

1. Draw a diagonal line from corner to corner on the wrong side of 18 print 2½" squares. Place each marked square right sides together with a second print square. Sew along the marked line. Trim ¼" from the line, and then press the seam allowances toward the darker fabric. Make 18 half-square-triangle units.

Make 18.

2. Sew together nine half-square-triangle units, making sure to orient all the seams in the same direction as shown. Press the seam allowances in one direction. Make two pieced strips, 2½" x 18½".

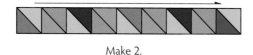

Make 2.

3. Sew red 2" x 18½" strips to the long edges of the pieced strips. Press the seam allowances as shown. Lay out the three navy rectangles alternating with the pieced segments. Sew the rectangles and segments together along the long edges to complete the outer-bag panel; press the seam allowances toward the red strips. The bag panel should be 18½" x 28½".

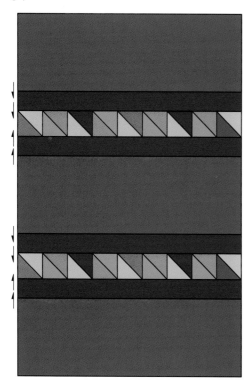

4. Fuse the interfacing rectangle to the wrong side of the outer-bag panel following the manufacturer's instructions. Fold the panel

in half widthwise with right sides together, and then sew the side seams.

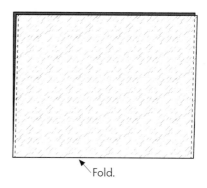

Fold.

Assembling the Lining

1. Fold one white print rectangle in half widthwise with right sides together. Sew the long open edge. Turn the rectangle right side out; press. It should now measure 8" x 18½". Make two pockets.

2. Place the aqua rectangle right side up. Center each pocket 2½" from the short edges of the rectangle; pin in place. Sew the inner edge of each pocket through both layers. To divide the pockets into smaller sections, sew a vertical line 6½" from each side.

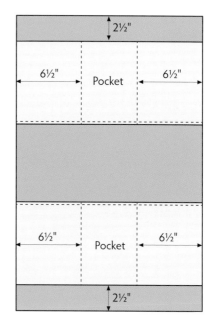

SEW THIS AND THAT!

3. Fold the lining in half widthwise with right sides together to make an 18½" x 14½" rectangle. Sew the side seams and leave the top open.

Finishing the Bag

1. Pinch the bottom corners of the outer bag with right sides together, matching the side seams and the center of the bottom of the bag to form a triangle. Sew across each triangle 2½" from the point. Repeat to box the bottom corners of the lining.

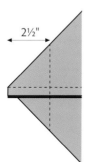

2½"

2. For the button loop, fold the long edges of the red 2" x 6½" strip toward the wrong side to meet in the center; press. Fold the strip in half again; press. Edgestitch the long edges. Fold the strip in half, aligning the short ends and forming a point at the folded end. Sew across the folded end to secure the point. Center the ends of the strip on the top edge of the bag on the right side. Baste the ends in place.

3. Turn the outer bag right side out. Place the lining inside of the outer bag with wrong sides together, matching the side seams and top edges. Use the red strips to make the binding. Use your preferred binding method to attach the red 2½"-wide strip to the top raw edges, or refer to "Timesaving Binding" on page 10.

4. Mark the outer bag 1¾" from the top edge and 5" from each side seam. Install a metal grommet at each mark, following the product manufacturer's instructions.

5. Fold the short edges of each red 4" x 33" strip ½" toward the wrong side; press. Fold the long edges toward the wrong side to meet in the center; press. Open one fold, and then place one piece of cotton webbing within the fold. Fold the strip in half lengthwise, enclosing the raw edges and the webbing. Topstitch around the perimeter of the strip. Make two handles.

6. Insert the handle ends through the grommets from the inside of the bag, and then knot the ends on the outside of the bag on each side.

7. Make the covered button according to the manufacturer's instructions. Hand sew the button to the front of the tote at the center of the top edge.

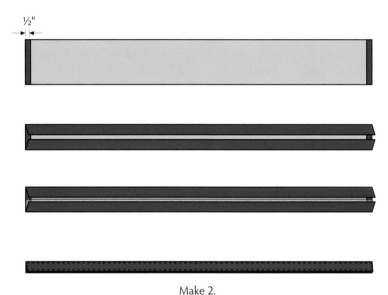

½"

Make 2.

SEW THIS AND THAT!

Sweet Stuff Pouch

Make a zippered pouch for all the little things you want to keep close at hand. A cute clutch is a great companion for any tote bag.

FINISHED SIZE: 6" x 6"

Materials

Yardage is based on 42"-wide fabric unless otherwise noted.

6 squares, 5" x 5", *total* of bright-pink, green, and aqua prints for outer pouch
⅛ yard of red print for outer pouch and top accent
1 fat eighth (9" x 21") of white print for lining
2½" x 9" strip of pink print for strap
18" x 22" rectangle of medium-weight fusible interfacing
9"-long all-purpose polyester zipper
¾"-diameter covered button kit and fabric scrap
Basting spray

Cutting

All measurements include ¼" seam allowances.

From *3* of the bright squares, cut:
6 rectangles, 2½" x 5"

From *3* of the bright squares, cut:
3 squares, 2½" x 2½"

From the red print, cut:
4 rectangles, 2½" x 7"
2 squares, 1¼" x 1¼"

From the white print, cut:
2 rectangles, 6" x 6½"

From the interfacing, cut:
2 rectangles, 2½" x 7"
1 rectangle, 6½" x 11½"

Preparing the Pouch Pieces

1. Sew three bright 2½" x 5" rectangles together along the long edges; press the seam allowances away from the center. Make two pieces, 5" x 6½". Sew three bright 2½" squares together; press the seam allowances toward the center square.

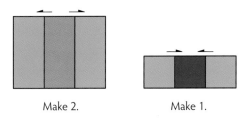

Make 2.   Make 1.

2. Sew the three-square unit to one short edge of a rectangle unit. Press the seam allowances toward the square unit. Sew the opposite edge of the square unit to the remaining rectangle unit; press. The unit should be 6½" x 11½".

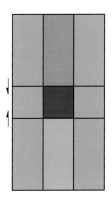

SEW THIS AND THAT!

3. Fuse the large interfacing rectangle to the wrong side of the pieced pouch panel following the manufacturer's instructions. Fuse the small interfacing rectangles to the wrong side of two of the red rectangles. Using the pattern on page 59, cut out four pouch tops from the red rectangles.

4. Place one interfaced pouch top right sides together with one pouch top without interfacing. Stitch the curved edge, leaving the sides and long straight edge open. Clip the curves up to, but not through, the stitching line. Turn the pouch-top unit right side out; press. Repeat to make two units.

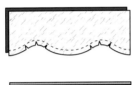

Make 2.

5. Fold the long edges of the pink 2½" x 9" strip toward the wrong side to meet at the center; press. Fold the strip in half lengthwise, enclosing the raw edges; press. Topstitch the long edges.

6. Fold each red 1¼" square in half; press. Place a square on the top end of the zipper, moving the zipper pull just below the fold. Topstitch the fold. Measure 6½" from the top of the zipper and place the remaining square over the zipper at this point. Sew the square in place, stitching carefully over the zipper teeth. Trim the excess zipper.

Topstitch.

Assembling the Pouch

1. Place the red top units on the short ends of the pouch with right sides facing up, aligning the straight edges. Fold the pink strap in half widthwise, and then place the raw ends along the right edge of the pouch, 1" from the top edge; pin in place. Baste the strap ends in place.

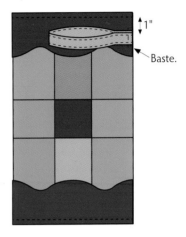

1"

Baste.

2. Place the zipper right side down along one short edge of the pouch. Baste the zipper tape in place using a ⅛" seam allowance.

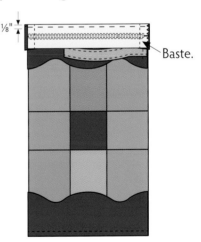

⅛"

Baste.

3. Place one of the white lining pieces right side down over the pouch, sandwiching the zipper. Sew the short edge through all layers.

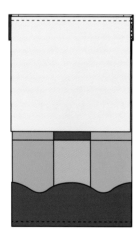

4. Fold the lining piece out of the way, and then fold the pouch to match the free zipper-tape edge to the opposite short edge of the pouch with right sides together. Repeat the process from steps 2 and 3, basting the zipper tape to the pouch and then attaching the remaining lining piece with right sides together.

5. Unzip the zipper halfway. Fold the lining pieces away from the pouch and align them with right sides together; pin. Sew the open edges of the pouch and lining, leaving a 3" opening in one edge of the lining for turning the pouch right side out.

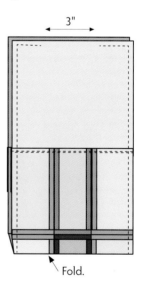

3"

Fold.

6. With the pouch still turned wrong side out, pinch the lower corners of the outer pouch, aligning the side seams with the bottom panel and forming a triangle. Stitch across each triangle 1¼" from the point. Repeat to box the lower corners of the lining. Trim the seam allowances of the boxed corners to ¼".

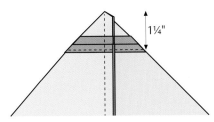

7. Turn the bag right side out through the opening in the lining. Hand or machine sew the opening closed, and then push the lining into the pouch; press.

8. Follow the manufacturer's instructions for the button kit to cover the button with a coordinating fabric scrap. Hand sew the button to the front of the pouch in the center of the pouch-top unit.

Zipper Tips

Projects that include a zipper can be a bit intimidating, but these helpful hints will take away your zipper-stitching stress.

- Zippers come in a variety of weights and materials. The best type of zipper for a small project like this pouch is one with lightweight plastic teeth. You can easily cut the through the teeth to trim the zipper. You can also stitch through the teeth without breaking your needle.

- Don't be shy about basting. Pins can be cumbersome when you're stitching a zipper, so it's often faster and easier to baste the zipper in place using the longest stitch length on your machine. Or try using narrow adhesive basting tape or even a regular glue stick for an even faster fix.

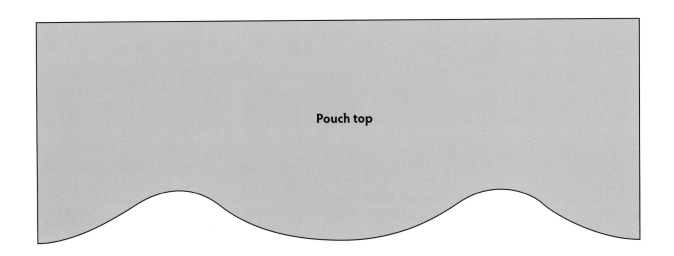

Pouch top

Evening Star Mini Quilt

Decorate a tabletop or wall with a lovely patchwork star. This small quilt is quick and easy to assemble from precut 5" squares.

FINISHED SIZE: 25" x 25"

Materials

Yardage is based on 42"-wide fabric unless otherwise noted.

16 squares, 5" x 5", of assorted red prints for hourglass and border units

12 squares, 5" x 5", of white print for background

10 squares, 5" x 5", of assorted green prints for four-patch and flying-geese units

8 squares, 5" x 5", of assorted medium-blue prints for center and corner units

6 squares, 5" x 5", of assorted yellow prints for four-patch units

2 squares, 5" x 5", of assorted navy prints for four-patch units

¼ yard of navy solid for binding

½ yard of fabric for backing

30" x 30" piece of batting

Cutting

All measurements include ¼" seam allowances.

From *8* of the white squares, cut:
8 squares, 4¾" x 4¾"

From *4* of the white squares, cut:
8 rectangles, 2¼" x 4"

From the yellow squares, cut:
24 squares, 2¼" x 2¼"

From the green squares, cut:
32 squares, 2¼" x 2¼"

From the red squares, cut:
8 squares, 4¾" x 4¾"
16 rectangles, 2¼" x 4"

From the medium-blue squares, cut:
8 squares, 4" x 4"

From the navy squares, cut:
8 squares, 2¼" x 2¼"

From the navy solid, cut:
3 strips, 2½" x 42"

Assembling the Quilt Center

1. Draw a diagonal line from corner to corner on the wrong side of the white 4¾" squares. Place a marked square right sides together with a red 4¾" square. Stitch ¼" from each side of the drawn line. Cut along the line to yield two half-square-triangle units. Press the seam allowances toward the red fabric. Make 16. The units should be 4¼" square.

Make 16.

4. Repeat step 3 to make four yellow/blue four-patch units.

5. Lay out four hourglass units, one yellow/blue four-patch unit, two yellow/green four-patch units, and two medium-blue squares in three rows of three as shown. Sew the units in each row together; press the seam allowances in opposite directions from row to row. Sew the rows together; press the seam allowances in one direction. Make four blocks, 11" square.

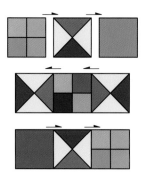
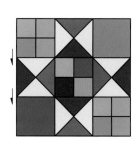

Make 4.

2. Draw a diagonal line perpendicular to the seam on the wrong side of eight half-square-triangle units. Place one marked unit right sides together with an unmarked unit, aligning the opposite fabric colors. Sew ¼" from each side of the drawn line. Cut along the line to yield two hourglass units. Press the seam allowances in one direction. Trim the hourglass units to 4" square. Make 16.

Make 16.

6. Sew the blocks together in two rows of two, rotating the blocks to position the blue squares at the center as shown. Press the seam allowances in one direction. The quilt center should be 21½" square.

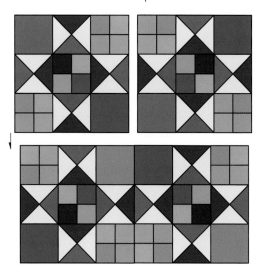

3. Lay out two yellow and two green 2¼" squares in two rows as shown. Sew the squares in each row together; press the seam allowances toward the green squares. Sew the rows together; press the seam allowances in one direction. Make eight yellow/green four-patch units, 4" square.

Make 8.

SEW THIS AND THAT!

Adding the Border

1. Draw a diagonal line from corner to corner on the remaining green squares. Place one green square on the end of one white rectangle with right sides together. Sew along the line. Trim the seam allowances to ¼", and then press toward the green corner. Repeat to sew a green square to the opposite end of the rectangle. Make eight flying-geese units, 2¼" x 4".

Make 8.

2. Lay out four red rectangles and two flying-geese units as shown. Sew the units together along the short edges; press the seam allowances in one direction. Make four border units, 2¼" x 21½".

Make 4.

3. Sew navy squares to the ends of two of the border units; press the seam allowances toward the squares. The units should be 2¼" x 25½".

Make 2.

4. Sew the border units without end squares to the sides of the quilt center; press the seam allowances toward the borders. Sew the remaining border units to the top and bottom of the quilt center; press.

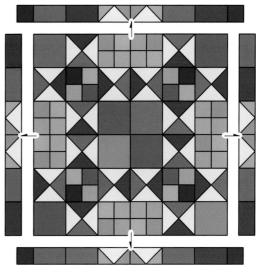

Quilt assembly

Finishing the Quilt

1. Layer the backing, batting, and quilt top. Baste the layers together. Hand or machine quilt as desired. The quilt shown was quilted with a stippling pattern in the background and an orange-peel design outlining the squares and rectangles.

2. Use the navy 2½"-wide strips to make the binding. Bind the quilt according to your preferred method, or refer to "Timesaving Binding" on page 10.

about the author

SHERRI K. FALLS is the designer of This & That Pattern Company. She began quilting in 1994 and enjoyed putting quilt patterns together in her own unique way, which inspired her to start experimenting with designing her own patterns.

In 2000, Sherri started a machine-quilting business with her mother, who owned a quilt store in scenic Waconia, Minnesota. It was at that store that she met Eileen Taylor, designer of the Holly Taylor fabric line from Moda Fabrics. When Eileen encouraged Sherri to create patterns for the Holly Taylor line in 2004, This & That Pattern Company was born. Since then, Sherri has designed many patterns and a book for the Holly Taylor fabric lines. She's also created fun patterns for charm packs, Jelly Rolls, and Layer Cakes under the Little Scraps and Breakfast Club lines.

Sherri has been married to her husband, Paul, for 25 years. They have two girls and a boy, ages 22, 18, and 16. You can visit Sherri at ThisandThatPatterns.com.

Acknowledgments

Many thanks to Moda Fabrics and Aurifil for generously providing project supplies.